Buckley & Ralphy
the Highland Cow   the Goat

A True Story about Kindness, Friendship, and Being Yourself

Photos by Leslie Ackerman | Written by Renee M. Rutledge

T0052734

BLOOM BOOKS
FOR YOUNG READERS

Published by:
ULYSSES PRESS
PO Box 3440
Berkeley, CA 94703
www.ulyssespress.com

ISBN: 978-1-64604-589-1 (paperback)
ISBN: 978-1-64604-028-5 (hardback)
Library of Congress Control Number: 2020931876

Printed in the United States
10 9 8 7 6 5 4 3 2 1

Acquisitions editor: Casie Vogel
Managing editor: Claire Chun
Editor: Julie Holland
Proofreader: Barbara Schultz
Cover design: Tobi Carter
Photographs: Leslie Ackerman
Illustrations: Natia Gogiashvili

To friends like Buckley and Ralphy,
who see each other through

Buckley the Highland calf loved the smell of fresh hay in the morning. He loved the sound of rain tapping on the slanted barn roof in the evening. But most of all, any time of day, Buckley loved the warm comfort of his mama.

Buckley believed the things he loved would never change. But one day, he woke up to find his mama gone. She had been sold to another farm.

Buckley was an orphan.

But Buckley didn't stay an orphan for long. When he was just five weeks old, Buckley was adopted by Leslie the rancher.

Leslie had known Buckley since he was one day old.

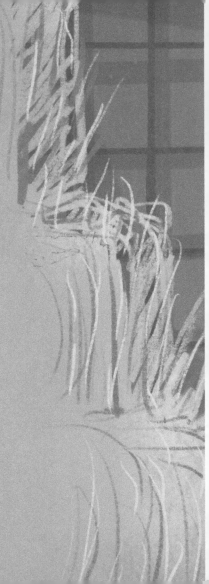

Leslie told Buckley that he was a special calf. His long, ginger-red fur would keep him warm through cold, rainy winters like those of the Highlands, the mountains of northern Scotland, where cows like him come from. Someday, she told him, Buckley would grow long, thick horns.

Leslie brought Buckley to live on her ranch with three goats, a puppy, a horse, two donkeys, and a pig.

Even though Buckley
had a warm pen of his
own, he felt so sad.
He cried all night in
his new home.

He missed his mama.

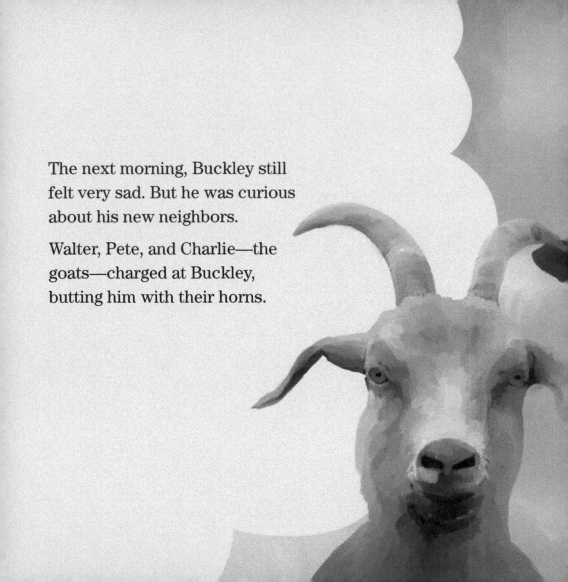

The next morning, Buckley still felt very sad. But he was curious about his new neighbors.

Walter, Pete, and Charlie—the goats—charged at Buckley, butting him with their horns.

Sam the puppy sniffed at Buckley then dashed away to chase a squirrel.

Saphy the horse stood straight and still, without so much as a whinny.

Penelope and Charlotte, the donkeys, just stared.

And Wally the pig oinked on his way to the feeding trough.

Buckley was too sad to eat. He left his feeder full. He lay in the same shady corner of the corral all day.

Leslie the rancher brought a bouncy red ball to cheer him up. But Buckley felt too lonely to play.

On the second night at Leslie's ranch, the dark sky blinked with stars, and an owl hooted in the nearby trees.

Buckley could not sleep without his mama. Again, he cried all night in his soft straw bed.

Buckley was sad for a long time. But then, one morning, something changed.

Leslie the rancher was standing in Buckley's corral. "I brought you a friend," she said, "so you won't feel alone."

Curious, Buckley sat up a little straighter in the straw and perked up his furry brown ears.

That's when he met Ralphy the Nubian kid. Leslie said that goats like Ralphy come from the Middle East and North Africa. Ralphy was seven weeks old, and he was an orphan just like Buckley!

Ralphy's fur was dark brown. His long ears, spotted white, dangled onto the sides of his face. They matched the white spot on his head.

Ralphy stayed in the same pen with Buckley. Leslie the rancher separated them with a thin fence while they got to know each other.

Just like Buckley, Ralphy was very sad on his first night at the ranch. He curled up in the back of the pen—away from the fence, away from Buckley—and went to sleep.

Buckley closed his eyes. For the first time, he didn't cry himself to sleep. He was too busy wondering about Ralphy.

The next day, Buckley and Ralphy kept each other company.

Buckley watched Ralphy eat his food and decided he would eat, too.

Buckley hadn't eaten in days. He was very hungry! Leslie the rancher watched him lick his feeder clean and even gave him seconds.

Leslie placed Buckley's feeder next to Ralphy's. From then on, they ate side by side.

At night, Buckley and Ralphy slept as close together as they could with the fence between them, so Leslie the rancher took it down. Now, Buckley and Ralphy could snuggle.

When the dark sky blinked with stars and the owl hooted in the nearby trees, Buckley felt safe and happy. He had his best friend beside him!

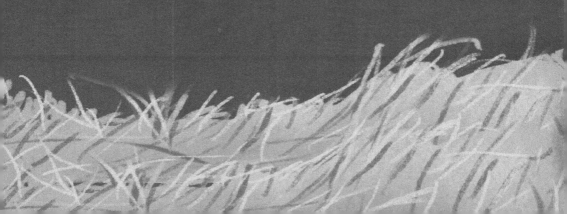

Buckley and Ralphy spent every day together in the barn. They were ready to explore! Wherever they went, they made sure to go together.

Buckley and Ralphy enjoyed getting to know new friends around the barnyard.

Penelope and Charlotte, the donkeys, grunted hello to Buckley and Ralphy through their white picket fence.

Wally the pig walked over a
little closer to them every day.

Running in circles around them,
Sam the puppy wagged his tail.

They could count on Saphy the horse
to share the food in her stall.

Buckley was afraid of Walter, Pete, and Charlie, the goats. They had butted him with their horns, and Buckley still remembered how that hurt.

Ralphy stood up to the other goats. He taught Buckley how to headbutt.

Headbutting became one of their favorite games.

Ralphy taught Buckley how to find food on the branches of the trees. They nibbled at leaves and tiny fruits.

Buckley showed Ralphy how to turn the empty feed bucket into a toy.

They shared their hay, grazed the pasture, and chewed their cud together all afternoon.

But Ralphy and Buckley didn't share everything. Buckley loved to splash and play outside in the rain while Ralphy stayed dry in the barn. Ralphy liked to show off his dance moves in the courtyard as Buckley watched.

No matter what, Ralphy and Buckley accepted each other—exactly as they were.

Sometimes Ralphy and Buckley got into trouble. Once, they zoomed around the courtyard and broke the gate. Another time, they chewed through an old saddle in the barn.

But when they were gentle, Leslie the rancher would reward them with treats. Grapes were their favorite!

One day, Buckley woke up to find Ralphy gone.

A painful foxtail weed had gotten stuck near Ralphy's eye.
Leslie the rancher placed him in a separate stall for the
veterinarian's visit.

Buckley did not stop mooing until he saw Ralphy again.

Over time, Buckley trusted that Ralphy would never go away for good. His friend would always come back to him.

When Buckley's hoof cracked, it was Ralphy's turn to worry. He stood tall by Buckley's side, protecting him.

Leslie the rancher took Buckley away to trim his hoof.

Ralphy waited patiently. He knew he could count on Buckley to return.

Both Buckley and Ralphy finished their food every day. They grew up quickly.

By the end of the summer, Buckley had doubled in size, towering over Ralphy. The tiny stumps of horns on Buckley's head grew long and thick, just like Leslie had said they would.

This didn't stop the friends from grazing the pasture together, rolling the bucket with their noses, bouncing Buckley's red ball, or zooming around the corral.

Now, when they played their favorite headbutting game, Buckley was extra gentle. He did not want to hurt Ralphy.

And when Walter, Pete, and Charlie tried to bully them, now Buckley was the one who stood up for Ralphy!

Buckley and Ralphy were no longer a calf and a kid.

They were Buckley the Highland cow and Ralphy the Nubian goat.

Even though they were all grown up, they stayed the best of friends.

And while Leslie's ranch was a warm and wonderful place, it was their friendship that made Buckley and Ralphy feel so happy there. They had found their home.

Pet Adoption Resources

Adopt a Pet • https://www.adoptapet.com
This searchable database of 17,000 animal shelters and rescues lists farm animals, horses, reptiles, amphibians, fish, birds, rabbits, dogs, and cats available for adoption.

Animal Place • https://animalplace.org/the-animals
A Grass Valley, California, sanctuary for cows, pigs, chicks, sheep, goats, and other animals, Animal Place also includes animals available for adoption.

The Cows Foundation • https://thecowsfoundation.org/adopt-a-cow
Offers a monthly sponsorship program for those who would like to contribute to the ongoing maintenance and health of a cow from one of many different farms and sanctuaries.

Farm Sanctuary • https://www.farmsanctuary.org
With locations in California, Maryland, Massachusetts, and New York, Farm Sanctuary rescues farm animals and offers a home adoption and placement service.

The Gentle Barn • https://www.gentlebarn.org/visit-our-location
With locations in California, Tennessee, and Missouri, The Gentle Barn teaches kindness and compassion for animals and runs an animal sponsorship program.

Goatlandia Sanctuary • https://www.goatlandia.org
This animal sanctuary rescues farm animals, provides a loving home for them, and places them in forever homes through an adoption program.

The International Society for Cow Protection • https://iscowp.org/adopt-a-cow
This group promotes compassionate cow protection by educating the public on alternatives to agricultural and dietary practices that depend on meat and dairy. The ISCOWP also offers a cow sponsorship program.

New Moon Farm Sanctuary • https://www.newmoonfarm.org
A peaceful sanctuary for rescued farm animals, New Moon Farm Sanctuary also provides an adoption and rehoming program.

NoKill Network • https://www.nokillnetwork.org
This site helps people locate adoptable pets from no-kill animal shelters, organizations, and rescue groups in every state.

Petfinder • www.petfinder.com
An online database of dogs, cats, horses, birds, barnyard animals, and other pets in need of adoption, searchable by area. Includes a directory of national animal shelters and pet adoption organizations.

About Leslie

Leslie has loved animals since she was a little girl, bringing home hurt birds and squirrels then raising and releasing them. She went on to college and got her veterinary technician degree in both Florida (where she grew up) and in California (where she lives now). A San Francisco Bay Area resident for 30 years, she was also a part-time zookeeper at an accredited zoo. On the side, she did wildlife rescue, specializing in raising and releasing raccoons. Once her three children were grown and moved from home, she and her husband, Cam, moved to a five-acre farm west of South Lake Tahoe. Here, Leslie was able to rescue and take in several farm animals, including Buckley. She continues to help with wildlife rescue, though her farm life keeps her very, very busy. You can follow Buckley and Ralphy's adventures on Instagram @Buckleythehighlandcow or Facebook @Buckley the Highland Cow.

About Renee

Renee's stories and articles about family, parenting, and the meaning of home have been widely published. She dedicated her award-winning novel, *The Hour of Daydreams*—a reimagined folktale—to her daughters, Maya and Raina. She is also the author of the children's books *One Hundred Percent Me* and *The ABCs of Asian American History*. When she isn't reading next to her tabby cat Storm, Renee loves adventuring, from hiking new trails to discovering hidden gems in small towns and big cities. Connect with her on Instagram @renee_rutledge or at www.reneerutledge.com.